To all

THOSE READY

and ready to live life on Purpose

Acknowledgments

There is no way to thank everyone who has helped shaped the woman I am now. This book is to everyone who has coached, advised, prayed, and taught me about life.

To my darling husband you are the best YES of my life and I am thankful everyday for letting you into my heart. With you I have found laughter, joy, and a reason to believe that God loves me.

To my siblings and my sons. Your words and laughter gives me the courage to keep reaching higher for greater. I love you all, now and always.

To my friend and business partner Olakitan Akinbamiro, they say good friends are hard to find, somehow we found each other. You have been such an incredible support through everything life had to offer.

To my mentor Taiwo Adepoju (the guardian of destinies), you have been a tree that I learn from daily. You have prayed with and for me, and I am grateful for the push to be better.

To my spiritual mentor Boma Shodeko, there is nothing that can explain the role you have played in my growth these past few years. Thank you for always supporting me.

To Sabbath Obot, knowing you has been a blessing. I thank God for you daily.

To Princess Olufemi, when I mentor you, I learn more about life and giving, and loving. I am awaiting the greatness already embedded in you.

To everyone else that has played a role or two in my life's journey, this book is for you. May you always find your YESortunities!

Table of Contents

Acknowledgements

The YES Factor..12
The Definition of YES..21
The Principle of YES..29
The Effect of a YES..39
The Secret of YES...51
What to say YES to...61
Saying YES can Change your Life....................................79

About the Author
Journal Workbook

The YES Factor

1
THE YES FACTOR

Always say 'yes' to the present moment... Surrender to what is. Say 'yes' to life - and see how life starts suddenly to start working for you rather than against you.
-Eckhart Tolle

I ONCE TOLD A CLIENT THOSE SAME WORDS! I TOLD HER IF YOU'D ASK ME TO BUILD A PLANE I'D SAY YES WITHOUT FLINCHING.

Not because I'm an aero engineer but because I said YES to life years ago.

After saying YES I would likely run to the nearest bookstore, buy a "How to build a Plane for Dummies", "An Idiots guide to building a plane", books and much more.

I would go online and start a Google search, and most importantly I would look for collaborators and build you the best plane my mind can conceive. It might take me a year or two or more, but you would get a plane that would fly across the world.

She smiled at me and nodded in agreement. My life is defined by the Yes's I had said. I said yes to love, and I am married to a beautiful man and gave birth to two incredible boys. I said YES to financial independence, and I'm now the CEO of my company. I said YES to creativity, and I can conceive with my mind whatever I'd like to create and make it happen. I'd said YES to God, and he has transformed my life.

Life is all about the choices we make, and they are all defined by the Yes's and No's we say daily. Life is essentially a choice and the word YES is the factor that determines the quality of that life. In my 15 years of talking to individuals about life, business, and building a brand, I have come to realize that the only ones who gets to live their dreams are the ones who said YES to new opportunities. The difference between that man and the other man sitting on the street corner is that the first man answered YES to every good opportunity that came along. He said yes to education, to a job, to an idea, to collaboration and much more.

An amazing thing happens when we begin to say YES to our dreams, they start to have life and take shape. Situations and events begin to align just because we said yes.

> *Life is all about the choices we make, and they are all defined by the Yes's and No's we say daily. Life is essentially a choice.*

Chances are that at some point in your life you have passed up an important opportunity to change your life. Chances are that you were too afraid to fail, that you denied yourself the opportunity to be happy and to live a full life.

I'm here to tell you that it isn't too late to start saying YES to living. The ideas that change our lives are sometimes very simple and not complex; those are the ideas that add a lifetime of value to our life.

Thomas Edison invested his time into creating a light bulb, even after he failed at it; he kept on working hard to make his dreams come through.

Only the ones that are determined to disrupt the status quo experience full lives. Saying YES is the factor that one needs to create a new business. Saying YES is the factor that inventors utilize to keep going at it.

Apple's CEO once said, "Here's to the crazy ones. The misfits. The rebels. The troublemakers. The round pegs in the square holes. The ones who see things differently. They're not fond of rules. And they have no respect for the status quo. You can quote them, disagree with them, glorify or vilify them. About the only thing, you can't do is ignore them. Because they change things. They push the human race forward. And while some may see them as the crazy ones, we see genius. Because the people who are crazy enough to think they can change the world are the ones who do."

Saying YES as birthed the most incredible fits. Technology that seemed like science fiction years ago is available to you and I because someone said YES to creating something amazing. I once posted the same quote on my Facebook page, and the response from a Mr. Bola Opere puts it in perspective. *"Most great men and women today didn't sit through life folding their arms. They saw an opportunity to do something, and they did. Thus, here's to*

PAGING and SALUTING Albert Einstein's Theory of Relativity, Sir. Isaac Newton's Law of Motion!, Madame Curie's Discovery of Uranium!, Thomas Edison's Electric Bulb, Henry Ford's Motor-Engine!, Enzo Ferrari's Racing Eccentricism!, Dr. Ferdinand Pierche's Porsche, Lamborghini's Speed Conjones, Rolls Jet-Engines!, Picasso's Abstract Expressionism!, Salvador Dali's Surreal Expressionism!, Jasper John's Modernism!, Mozart & Beethoven's Classics!, Shakespeare's Literary " Tragi-Comedies" & Romanticism!, Mahatma Gandhi's Dogged & Passive Freedom Resistance!, Martin Luther King's Civil Rights Movement!, Malcolm X's Righteous Indignation & Defiance!, President Roosevelt's NEW DEAL!, " OBAMA'S HOPE"-ful Post-Racist America!, Sir. Winston Churchill's War-Time Decisiveness That Saved Modern England from Hitler's Blitzerag, Sigmund Freud's Psychology, etc."

You can be one of them too. An elite set of individuals, not all of them are famous, but nonetheless, they have impacted lives in their little way.

No matter the circumstances surrounding your birth- your mom and dad said YES to conceiving you. Your mom said YES to giving birth to YOU. She said YES to sending you to school although she had a choice of saying NO. YES guides your entire existence, and even your choice to pick up this book is a perfect example.

This book will give you the guts you need to start living, by saying YES. You can recognize the opportunities and things to say YES to and the once to say NO to.

You are about to begin a journey that can substantially change your life and make you part of a clan of great men and women who have found the freedom in YES. In the words of President Barack Obama "YES WE CAN", and we did; three words that won over the world. You can win over your world through the same word.

The key to the YES philosophy is the ability to recognize opportunities and say YES to them. Opportunities presents themselves to us daily, you have to seek to recognize them when they knock. I don't believe that opportunity knocks but once, I do believe it knocks, once, twice, thrice etc. The perfect opportunity is usually the first to knock. You must be guided by the drive that sets men apart.

You must not live on dreams alone, because it's never enough. You must say YES to working your dreams and turning them into reality. You must have faith in your creative ability and utilize it.

In my upcoming book, **I MAKE SHIFT HAPPEN**, I outlined the story of my journey into creating and inventing. I also shared the secrets to idea generation and innovation and how you should have an idea book that would help you come up with great business ideas. I share the secrets of idea generation, idea banking, and idea refinement. As an innovation strategist, part of my job is to shift the paradigm of an organization or individual and help them maximize their potential.

Everyone is creative; everyone has dreams, and ideas. The one factor that sets the doers and successful people apart is the YES FACTOR; which is the basis for this small book.

The
DEFINITION
of Yes

2

THE DEFINITION OF YES

"Love is a place
& through this place of
love move
(with brightness of peace)
all places
yes is a world
& in this world of yes live
(skillfully curled)
all worlds"
— E.E. Cummings

IN HIS NEW YORK TIMES BESTSELLER BOOK, 'THE BOOK OF AWAKENING", Mark Nepo puts it beautifully and I quote, "In the face of this gritty, mysterious, and ever-changing dynamic we call being alive, it's nothing short of heroic that we are asked to choose life and living, again and again. Not just to put a good face on things while we're here, but because saying yes to life is how the worm inches its way through the earth. It's how salmon leap their way upstream. It's how flowers grow out of stone."

The whole of creation was made because God said YES to creating something out of utter darkness. Even in the grimmest of situations saying YES to a new perspective can change your world. If plants and animals have no other choice but to say yes to their existence and their role in the ecosystem; why not you?

I invite you to reflect on times in your life where you said YES to an opportunity, a meeting, a date, a lunch, an event, collaboration, and an idea. How did it transform your life? Did it change you? Did your existence evolve?

Saying YES to a meeting with a lady I met on meetup.com opened up one of the greatest opportunity of my life. I remember e-mailing Christy, and we decided to meet up at Rice Village for coffee. After a cup of latte and a blueberry muffin, she connected me with a company that would later help me bring my invention to life, a bio technology product. That one YES created a snowball of other events that ended up changing my life.

In August 2013, I had an idea for a product, which I sent to **As seen on TV**, they loved it, called me and we started the process of manufacturing the product. Although, the project is on hold; this example still speaks to the power of YES. In 2012, I also said YES to writing a book about sex and the teenage experience titled "READY? SEX? WAIT!, that book eventually opened the door to a movie production still in the works.

I have so many examples in my life to show you the power of YES. I have experienced moments of great highs and the opportunity to meet smart people because of the same word. I have been able to travel to amazing places and met amazing individuals because of it.

> "...saying yes to life is how the worm inches its way through the earth. It's how salmon leap their way upstream. It's how flowers grow out of stone."
>
> Mark Nepo

Growth occurs with every right choice (YES) we make. Our growth in life is tied to what we feed on, what we yield ourselves to. We are limited by our mindsets and how far we can utilize the power of YES.

I have never tried looking for the definition of YES until I decided to write this book. According to thefreedictionary.com, YES means it is so; as you say or ask. It is used to *express affirmation, agreement, consent, approval, positive confirmation, or consent.*

1. **An affirmative or consenting reply.**
2. **An affirmative vote or voter.**

It can be used to express great satisfaction, approval, or happiness.

Essentially, saying YES to living is the key to living a productive, unrestricted life. An unrestricted life is that life of constant quest and inhibited by the naysayers. Saying YES is expressing affirmation to doing the extraordinary and looking for new opportunities. Doing the extraordinary is being able to look for a problem and solve, is been the best at whatever you do, being extraordinary is defying the odds, and shunning mediocrity.

Saying YES means you are in agreement to live a full life of wonder. Saying YES is consenting to failure or success; and not being afraid of where the chips might fall.

Until we can define a thing, it might elude us. Until we can say assuredly what something is, we may never understand it. The best path to happiness is saying YES, we will talk about happiness in the next few chapters.

If you are like me, I have two little boys, and whenever I'd say YES to them doing something they love- their face would light up and they become super excited.

The same way your hearts light up as you give yourself the YES THERAPY and allow your soul to be free. You feed your heart with a constant dose of happiness.

A wish is only a wish until it's put in action. An idea is just an idea until it comes to fruition. The YES THERAPY is the ingredient to lasting happiness. I cannot emphasize it enough. It is the dream you say YES to that becomes reality. Saying YES to a new business idea can change your life; it can transform your circle and connect you with incredible people. Saying YES is the driving force of all I do. I don't just say YES to everything or everyone. Understanding the meaning of YES and its effect on my life as guided me to prioritize what do say YES to, when to say YES, and to whom or what.

The PRINCIPLE Of Yes

3

THE PRINCIPLE OF YES

"Probably some of the best things that have ever happened to you in life, happened because you said yes to something. Otherwise things just sort of stay the same."
— **Danny Wallace, Yes Man**

WHEN I ASK YOU TO SAY YES TO LIFE, I DON'T MEAN ADOPTING A LIFE OF ALWAYS BELIEVING THAT THE grass is always greener on the other side. Neither am I saying that all you need to do is think positive, and life would be hunky dory. Saying yes is not about creating your reality as some might teach. Creating your life depletes it of wonder, and mystery; it makes life unexciting and less mythological.

Our lives are not always shaped by the situations we knowingly create; they are shaped by circumstances we said YES to. Saying yes to a church member to help her distribute flyers at an office building, ushered me into finding love. When I met with her that cold winter day, love was the last thing on my mind. Then I met him; my husband to be, and I knew it was him. Saying YES to him birthed the idea of becoming a mommy. All of these events happened not because I planned it but because there is nothing in life that happens because of our Will. We may exercise our WILL all we want, but our WILL's are subject to divinity and wonder.

A more realistic and liberating viewpoint is this; while we can't control our life's events, we can control how we respond to them. When you say yes to life, you're saying yes to whatever comes your way.

I am reminded of a story I read some years ago of a woman who woke up with three strands of hair left on her head she decided to braid it, and she had an incredible day. The next day she woke up with two strands of hair; she decided to part it, and she had an amazing day. The next morning she woke up with one strand of hair, so she decided to put it in a ponytail, and she had an amazing day. She woke up and noticed she had no hair left on her head she said thank God, now I don't have to bother about doing something to my hair again. **YOUR ATTITUDE IS ALL THAT MATTERS!** She couldn't control the loss of her hair, but she was able to control her attitude.

> *Our lives are not always shaped by the situations we knowingly create; they are shaped by circumstances we said YES to.*

Saying yes to life means saying yes to change. Change is inevitable, it's preordained. Children are born, people die, people change, things change, etc. Life is all about change. The weather changes constantly and we don't even think about it. My life changed drastically in 2014, my business was plummeting, my finances depleted, a gained weight, lost relationships, had a minor heart attack and so much more. The change was massive, and it was a huge blow to my ego and my life. I stepped back from this fairy tale life I had setup and decided to let it die. I had to fail, so I can learn how to win. I decided that whatever doesn't make it through the fire is not meant to be. So I sat back and watched it burn. Whatever didn't make it through the fire wasn't worth holding onto. It gave me an opportunity to rebrand myself and change my perception about success.

As Howard H. Stevenson a Harvard Fellow once said in his speech titled "Building a Life", he said "balance sheets are not published in obituaries"; success is more than the money in our accounts, and how much fame we have. It is defined by the lives we've touched.

I had pivoted my standard of success to be how much I had in my account and by the age of 36; it wasn't happening fast enough. Even with a new start-up valuated to be over $50 million; I was depressed because it wasn't happening fast enough.

Change activates growth. I had gone through a lifetime in one year, and I felt I was losing the battle. Change is part of saying YES. Saying YES to the process of change because life can be messy at times, it can be uncertain, and uncomfortable. Saying yes to life means accepting that death is the only constant in life, and not only physical death but death to unproductive ventures, and relationships.

I'm a fan of Rascal Flakes, a country group with a song that says, "God Bless the Broken Road that Led me Straight to you."

There is always a broken road, and life's triumphant moments are preceded by pain and grief. Walt Disney was deemed unimaginative and was fired from his job. He later started Disney, one of the most imaginative companies of all time. Our victories in life can sometimes be borne out of great grief and loss.

Saying no to a bad relationship activates your meeting of Prince Charming; saying no to poverty activates the power to make wealth, saying no to mediocrity, activates to power of innovation and creativity.

Saying yes to change means saying yes to a continuum of feelings activated by change; which may include death or rebirth ranging from grief, uncertainty, fear, vulnerability, loneliness, doubt, confusion, discomfort, longing, excitement, hope, creativity, laughter.

Saying yes to life means saying yes to evolving and experiencing life in a new dimension. We have been burdened with the power to make choices and my life, and your life is ruled by it. We cannot run from it.

After I had spent a whole year depressed, and emotionally drained, I decided my growth was dependent on my taking some time off to refuel and reflect. I took a 60 days sabbatical to do this, but the first 30 days I spent talking myself out of it. I used to think that the point of spiritual growth was to eradicate fear and other crazy unspiritual feeling I was wrong.

Taking 60 days to refuel wasn't a mission to perform an exorcism on myself; nor was it to save myself from the feelings of dejection, hopelessness, and fear. Because like most people I have evolved, and I have mastered the art of containing those feelings, so it doesn't rule me. These people have said yes to living life despite those feelings and pursuing their dreams in spite of it all.

The most difficult moments of our lives are usually our greatest teachers. So I said YES to learning about myself, my calling, and my role on earth. I used the information I gathered to transform my brand and refocus. I would tell you one thing, greatness is born suddenly, like gold it passes through extreme fire and then it's awakened. But you have to say YES to the fire first.

Pema Chodron says it touchingly in her book **"When Things Fall Apart: Heart Advice for Difficult Times"**:

When we first begin our exploration, we have all kinds of ideals and expectations. We are looking for answers to satisfy a pang of hunger we have felt for a very long time. But the last thing we want is a further introduction to the boogeyman. Of course, people do try to warn us. "I remember when I first received meditation instruction, the woman told me the technique and guidelines on how to practice and then said, but please don't go away from here thinking that meditation is a vacation from irritation."

No one ever tells us to stop running away from fear. We are very rarely told to move closer, to just be there, to become familiar with fear. I once asked the Zen master Kobun Chino Roshi how he related with fear and he said, "I agree. I agree." But the advice we usually get is to sweeten it up, smooth it over, take a pill, distract ourselves, but by all means, make it go away.

So the next time you encounter fear, death, discouragement, loss, and failure, consider yourself lucky. You now have a shot at greatness; you have the chance for a do over. This is where the courage comes in. Usually, we think that brave people have no fear. The truth is that they are intimate with fear. They have mastered it and rule over it with grandeur that can't be defined. They are aware of possible failure but are not hinder by it.

> *The most difficult moments of our lives are usually our greatest teachers. So I said YES to learning about myself, my calling, and my role on earth.*

The EFFECT Of a Yes

4

THE EFFECT OF A YES

"Say yes and you'll figure it out afterwards."
— **Tina Fey**

LAST YEAR, IN THE MIDDLE OF MY SABBATICAL, I FOUND MYSELF INDULGING IN NEGATIVITY OF HOW horrible my life had turned out. For someone with a vast array of accomplishments I had set such a high standard and was afraid to fail. So I hid my face in shame once my business slowed down drastically; I had to ask for help which meant feeling vulnerable. I reacted with aversion to every facet of life around me.

My toddler had gotten Ring Worm from school passed it to his little brother, and then I got it. I showed my skin to everyone that cared to pay attention. It was embarrassing. Nothing was going right, especially me. Tired of the repugnance, I decided that instead of resisting everything and complaining about the cards I was dealt; I would begin to greet whatever arose with a YES, which came in the form of "it is well". I was not going to complain about it; I would see the beauty in it. Although my situation didn't change drastically, my attitude about it did.

I recently read a story online by an unknown author about the parable of the marbles; once upon a time, there was a foolish boy who had a bag full of beautiful marbles. Now this boy was quite proud of his marbles. In fact, he thought so much of them that he would neither play with them himself nor would he let anyone else play with them.

He only took them out of the bag in order to count and admire them; they were never used for their intended purpose. Yet that boy carried that coveted bag of marbles everywhere he went.

Well, there was also a wise boy who wished he could have such a fine bag of marbles. So this boy worked hard and earned money to purchase a nice bag to hold marbles. Even though he had not yet earned enough with which to purchase any marbles, he had faith and purchased the marble bag.

He took special care of the bag and dreamed of the day it would contain marbles with which he could play and share with his friends.

Alas, the foolish boy with all of the marbles didn't take care of the marble bag itself, and one day the bag developed a hole in the bottom seam. Still, he paid no attention and, one by one, the marbles fell out of the bag.

It didn't take long, once the foolish boy's marble bag developed a hole, for the wise boy to begin to find those beautiful marbles, one at a time, lying unnoticed on the ground. And, one by one, he added them to his marble bag. The wise boy thus gained a fine bag full of marbles in no time at all. This boy played with the marbles and shared them with all of his friends.

And he always took special care of the bag so he wouldn't lose any. Because the foolish boy was selfish and careless, he lost all of his marbles and was left holding the bag. The story thought me about appreciating life and the gifts I've been blessed with.

So I said YES to the ringworm, to the plummeting business, to the debt, to the shame, to the fear, I said YES to the pain. Slowly, my emotions began to change, and although my situation didn't change drastically, my attitude about it changed.

> *I would begin to greet whatever arose with a YES, which came in the form of "it is well". I was not going to complain about it; I would see the beauty in it.*

At first, my Yes was just a religious exercise, it was mechanical and insincere, but I noticed that after-a-while it began to change me. I'd gone on this long journey that kept me away from my interest and dreams. I'd spent about six months away from writing, speaking, blogging, singing, cooking, and designing. I had lost interest in the simplest things. I went on the journey, not by choice but time and life's issues overshadowed my very sense of self, and I completely lost that which made me, ME. I'd lost myself in bits, daily, to the perils of existence; to responsibilities, adulthood, to life.

So I chose happiness over fear and depression. My life was okay. I was exactly where I needed to be. The effect of YES makes living bearable even when the odds are against you. It makes your journey mythological.

I had lost the wonder of life and running a new business. I remembered days when going to church and playing drums was fun, when staying up late, cleaning and decorating the sanctuary was my oasis. I remember the percolating smell of trying out new gourmet recipes from the food network and how that thrilled me. I also remembered using my God given hands to design clothes, make gel candles that last for years. I remembered my voice, the sound of it, the use of it, I remembered the days the resounding of my voice broke a bulb in church. I remembered using my mind to create, and my fingers wrote passionate poems and how writing was my life. I remembered the inspiration, the tingle I felt when I wrote something new. I remembered the ideas, the dreams, the sense of ownership, the certainty of greatness, the knowing of who I am, and who was called to be.

> *For you to grow, you have to change your perception. You have to find wisdom and marry it, be one with it.*

Yea, life did happen, principles did somehow change, did things I never thought I could do, experienced feelings I never thought were possible but I believed in a new Genesis. I believed in the effect of YES. So one day, it happened, I had said YES long enough, and my being confirmed it.

I am now on a different journey; it just started. This is my first writing in 3 months; I am now pregnant with words, with stories yearning to be told, with ideas born out of adversity, with a new sense of self. My conflicted soul is now finding rest, who I once was and who I am now is a beautiful story, and teaches a great lesson. I am ready to come alive; I am prepared to bask in the wooing of the call.

That is the effect of YES. You can turn your situation around through your thought and by putting into effect things that can benefit your life.

For you to grow, you have to change your perception. You have to find wisdom and marry it, be one with it. Life can be complex, but that's the beauty of life. It makes for a great story when one that was homeless now makes millions, when one that was barren, now has children, when one that was on drugs, now is clean. It provides the awe and wonder that we all love and cheer for.

Difficult times have helped me to understand better than before, how infinitely rich and beautiful life is in every way, and that so many things that one goes worrying about are of no importance whatsoever... ~Isak Dinesen

I would end this chapter by sharing some steps to happiness as I learned over the years. This is the principle that guides my life; this is the lesson that has helped me through extremely trying times. I have learned my strengths which are quite awesome by the way. I have learned my limitations, and uniqueness. This is a tribute to the effect of yes, and the power it brings.

Everybody Knows
You can't be all things to all people.
You can't do all things at once.
You can't do all things equally well.
You can't do all things better than everyone else.
Your humanity is showing just like everyone else's.

So
You have to find out who you are, and be that.
You have to decide what comes first, and do that.
You have to discover your strengths, and use them.
You have to learn not to compete with others,
Because no one else is in the contest of being you.

Then
You will have learned to accept your own uniqueness.
You will have learned to set priorities and make decisions.

You will have learned to live with your limitations.

You will have learned to give yourself the respect that is due.

And you'll be a most vital mortal.

Dare To Believe

That you are a wonderful, unique person.

That you are a once-in-all-history event.

That it's more than a right, it's your duty, to be who you are.

That life is not a problem to solve, but a gift to cherish.

And you'll be able to stay one up on what used to get you down.

The SECRET Of Yes

5

THE SECRET OF YES

"I imagine that yes is the only living thing."
— E.E. Cummings

SAYING YES REQUIRES UNDERSTANDING THE SECRET OF THE WORD, YES. YEARS AGO, A BOOK CAME out named the "Secret", people wanted to know the secret to life but in order to know the secret of life you have to know the secret to saying YES to life. Saying yes is the way nature births itself without a cue from anyone. You may not notice, but everything in nature is governed by the YES principle. Animals and plants go through constant change. They have been around for more than 3 billion years ago and have evolved, coped, or suffered extinction. We have a lot to learn from them. This leads me to the next topic: What are you saying yes to?

WHAT ARE YOU SAYING YES TO?

This book is not encouraging you to say yes to everything and everyone; it's equipping you with the tools needed to determine what to say yes to.

Saying yes is the way nature births itself without a cue from anyone.

Some years ago, I'd say yes to everything, everyone, and every opportunity. I would say yes to a friend and later complain about it. I would say yes to a project that ends up stressing my life beyond measure. Some opportunities are great but not always great for you.

You have to decide what you are saying yes to. I have talked about the YES factor, the principle and the effect of YES but beyond those two we have to determine the secret to YES.

Think about how you learned how to write, first you had to understand your ABC's, and then your phonetics, and then your sight words. Once you understood the basics and how they work, you were ready to start writing. It's the same principle with YES.

When you begin the journey of not trying to control your life but to say YES to opportunities that are in line with your purpose then you can begin to understand how to implement the power in your life. Understanding your purpose is the basis for what you say yes to. Your YES's has to be in line with your calling. Knowing who you are guides your choices in life. You cannot be misguided by frivolous promises or quick fixes.

WHAT DOES SAYING YES FEELS LIKE?

Most of us have moments of great excitement that is a result of good occurrences. When we say yes to new things, new things come into our lives. This is not magic. Saying yes to going to graduate school earns you a Master's degree, and then a better-paying job, followed by a better income, a new living arrangement, and the list goes on. Things begin to work in sequential form; a snowball effect of some sort.

Saying YES to starting a business transformed my life, it awarded me opportunities that I wouldn't have otherwise. I had a sense of accomplishment, of pride, and independence.

SO WHAT IS THE SECRET REALLY?

The secret is no secret. The secret to YES is the utilization of it.

You have to begin today. Look at the situation you are in, and say YES to change it. Learn a new skill, go back to school, network, market your business, write a book, start a new job, change careers, say YES to meeting new people, and to breaking up with superficial friends. You cannot create your end-result in life, but you can say YES to possibilities.

Look at the situation you are in, and say YES to change it.

All of our dreams are enveloped inside our minds, and it can take flight as soon as we begin to let go of fear and embrace the change that exploration would bring.

A new life isn't elusive, it's not for the well privileged alone, and it's for you and I. Transformation only happens to those who are pliable enough and vulnerable, those willing to fight for change, those willing to open the gates to purpose.

You have to soar through life. Don't let your background, or limitations hold you back. There is nothing like limitation; it's all in your mind. You have to conquer your fears, and live a life of possibilities. You have to roar through life. Not timidly but with great strength. As kings and queens not like mere men.

An author once wrote: I woke up early today, excited over all I get to do before the clock strikes midnight. I have responsibilities to fulfill today and I am important. My job is to choose what kind of day I am going to have.

Today I can complain because the weather is rainy or I can be thankful that the grass is getting watered for free.

Today I can feel sad that I don't have more money or I can be glad that my finances encourage me to plan my purchases wisely and guide me away from waste.

Today I can grumble about my health or I can rejoice that I am alive.

Today I can lament over all that my parents didn't give me when I was growing up or I can feel grateful that they allowed me to be born.

Today I can cry because roses have thorns or I can celebrate that thorns have roses.

Today I can mourn my lack of friends or I can excitedly embark upon a quest to discover new relationships.

Today I can whine because I have to go to work or I can shout for joy because I have a job to do.

Today I can complain because I have to go to school or eagerly open my mind and fill it with rich new tidbits of knowledge.

Today I can murmur dejectedly because I have to do housework or I can appreciate that I have a place to call home.

Today stretches ahead of me, waiting to be shaped. And here I am the sculptor who gets to do the shaping.

What today will be like is up to me. I get to choose what kind of day I will have!

What
TO SAY YES
to

6

WHAT TO SAY YES TO

"If somebody offers you an amazing opportunity but you are not sure you can do it, say yes – then learn how to do it later!"
— **Richard Branson**

YOU NOW KNOW THE SECRET OF YES, THE DEFINITION, AND THE PRINCIPLE OF IT. Now I need to teach you what to say yes to. Four months ago I taught this principle to a friend who met a guy she liked on Facebook but she was afraid to initiate a conversation. I nudged her to add him, and sure enough he said hello. To her surprise, they started talking and have been dating ever since.

It's easy to say everything we say yes to ends up great but sometimes they don't. The fact is life isn't promised to be without pain. I am elated whenever I see individuals saying yes to living life. I am not talking about living life in recklessness because every choice we make carries with it consequences, irreparable ones that never goes away; choices that are laced with regrets.

I have said YES plenty of times to things that ended up badly. I looked at those things as lessons that needed to be learned. I learned how to forgive, and how to love from bad experiences.

I built my brand and business by saying YES to becoming my own boss. The life I have now albeit imperfect is a life I said YES to. You can never hide from life because you want everything about your existence to be perfect.

So let me ask you this one question: **IF FAILURE WASN'T AN OPTION OR DIDN'T EXIST, WHAT WOULD YOU BE DOING WITH YOUR LIFE?**

Now let's go! Failure does not exist! It is illusive!

No one fails or is a failure. Failure only exists in the minds of people who spend time comparing. My business didn't fail; the doors needed to be closed so that something better, something new can come into my life. Essentially what people call failure is CHANGE; a death and rebirth, of life and dreams.

You can never hide from life because you want everything about your existence to be perfect.

So again, if failure wasn't an option or didn't exist, what would you be doing with your life right now?

I would say yes to a trip around the world, an invention to help people live a more productive life, a career in music, and a gourmet restaurant. Those would be some of my options but then again, my life is full of wonder as it is that I don't necessarily yearn for a career in music as much as I yearn for inventions to change lives.

SO WHAT DO YOU SAY YES TO?

SAY YES TO OPPORTUNITIES

Say Yes to opportunities in business. As I mentioned earlier, when I had an idea to invent a Biotechnology product for women, I filed for a patent and then connected with a stranger via meetup who went on to change my life. If I had spent years contemplating the possibilities of failure, then I wouldn't have changed my life.

If I had looked at how unqualified I was in that spectrum, I would have spent time dodging the idea and looking for an easier invention. Becoming an inventor involves a YES attitude. That it can be done, type of spunk! You have to look daily for ways to make life easier for the people around you. Disrupt the way things are done by changing it positively. Take that promotion at work if its line with your purpose. Go on that trip to unwind if it fits your budget, partner with your mom if that helps birth a lifelong dream for you, and make you both closer. Move back home if that would help you save up for your home.

Don't look at others to determine your path in life. Work out your path and only measure your success by the standards you have set for yourself.

SAY YES TO FINANCIAL FREEDOM

Saying yes to financial freedom involves looking for ways to get out of debt, ways to make money, etc. Find out what you are good at, see if it's marketable, and then sell it. I recently spoke at Prairie View A& M University on "Ideas to Cash", where I taught students how to turn their ideas into money making ventures, how to create ideas, and find a market for their products.

My friend is very good at money management, when others called her stingy; she went to school to study accounting. Beyond that, she started an accounting company helping individuals and small businesses manage their finance. She needed more time at home with her kids so starting a business would help her accomplish that. Not all of us will become millionaires, but we can indulge in financial freedom by saying Yes to changing our lives.

SAY YES TO LEARNING

Learning is not limited to formal education. Learning involves what I call **STREET EDUCATION**, learning that which can't be taught in school. The principles of life aren't always taught in classrooms. We learn as we go through life. Although I have never been in the streets, I have learned a lot albeit a little late; about life by listening to others. You have to learn how to cope; you have to learn that life ain't fair. Street education teaches you that nobody cares if you get stiffed, or how hungry you are. You have to learn that in the end, you are on your own. You have to fight to protect your purpose and your dreams. These lessons will teach you that everybody's trying to get a piece of the action, trying to survive.

You can learn a lot from books, but it's not always enough; you could end up like Claudius, the wisest idiot in Rome. Life is like the street. One minute you can be on top and the coolest cat on the block. The next minute you are ambuscaded and shot in the butt. All of a sudden your business, family, health, or divorce, can turn your debutant life upside down.

The other type of learning is **SPIRITUAL EDUCATION**, learning from formal religion, doctrine, and precepts. Following the moral compass set by religion and having something that keeps your heart aligned, something that gives you hope. Beyond this two we should always opt to learn through **FORMAL EDUCATION**; to sharpen our skills, make ourselves more marketable in the job market. Get a degree, take courses online, read books, get certified in a certain skill.

SAY YES TO LOVE

I told you earlier the sequential events that led to me meeting my husband. By opening up, my heart gave me the chance to love. Most people are afraid to receive love and give love. I once heard, that the love you give, is the love you receive. You have to say YES to love, to meeting new people, to taking chances, to moving on even when you have been hurt before. Love is the most serene feeling in the world; it opens you up to the possibility of forever.

Keep this in mind: "A house becomes a home when you can write 'I love you' on the furniture. I can't tell you how many countless hours that I have spent cleaning. I used to spend at least 8 hours every weekend making sure things were just perfect - 'in case someone came over.' Then I realized one day that no-one came over; they were all out living life and having fun!

Now, when people visit, I find no need to explain the condition of my home. They are more interested in hearing about the things I've been doing while I was away living life and having fun. If you haven't quite figured this out as yet, please heed this advice.

Life is short, so enjoy it! Dust if you must, but wouldn't it be better to paint a picture or write a letter, bake a cake or plant a seed, or even ponder the difference between want and need? Dust if you must, but there's not much time, with rivers to swim and mountains to climb, music to hear and books to read, friends to cherish and life to lead. Dust if you must, but the worlds out there with the sun in your eyes, the wind in your hair, a flutter of snow, and a shower of rain. This day will not come around again.

Dust if you must, but bear in mind, old age will come and it's not kind. And when you go - and go you must, you, yourself will make more dust! It's not what you gather, but what you scatter that tells what kind of life you have lived ... and remember a layer of dust protects the wood beneath it.

SAY YES TO GOD

I believe in a God who deals with the affairs of men. I said YES to serving him because He touches my heart in ways no one else would. Most people frown on organized religion because of control they seem to lose. I tell people to seek a relationship with God, not a religion. The spirit of God will hover over you, and His wisdom will envelope you. Say YES to

God, love, and life. Every day you will learn something new, about love, about God and your purpose.

SAY YES TO HAPPINESS

A quote written by Martha Washington says, "I am determined to be cheerful and happy in whatever situation I may find myself. For I have learned that the greater part of our misery or unhappiness is determined not by our circumstance but our disposition". You have to find your happiness. As a little girl, I kept wondering what fun was, or what happiness felt like. Laughing does not necessarily mean happiness; I can smile and be unhappy. Happiness is that deep feeling within that defers any outward occurrence. It's finding joy within. It comes from saying YES to living, to love, to God. We could be happy if we chose to be. Just like saying YES can be a compound effect, happiness is a compound effect.

> *The principles of life aren't always taught in classrooms. We learn as we go through life.*

SAY YES TO GOOD HEALTH

Without good health whatever we say YES to is temporary. We have to be determined to be healthy. In the book, "Take Charge of your Health" Pastor K.B. Sanusi, writes "To start with, you cannot prevent any disease if you lack knowledge of how your body works. If you're willing to spend time learning how to monitor your bank statement, sign your lease agreement, earn your degree, then you should be able to devote some time to learn about how your body functions."

Learning to say YES to good health means, giving your body the proper nutrients, nourishing it, and taking care of it. It means learning to slow down, refuel, and rest. A principle I had to learn the hard way and working non-stop on.

HOW TO SAY YES

Rather than a mechanical chant of YES that some gurus teach, saying YES doesn't have a formula; it's something that should come from within. It is believing. Transformations can only happen when we say yes to opportunities life offers.

The principle of faking it till you make, can be utilized in this instance. Start by writing down your life's purpose and then start journaling things and experiences you'd like to see on your journey; then say YES to them. It's that simple. If you'd like to work for a financial institution and it requires a master's degree in accounting. You would have to say YES to a master's degree. If you'd like to start a restaurant and you have no cooking skill, you would start by taking some cooking classes.

My cousin wanted to someday work in the White House, so she went to law school, volunteered for the Obama campaign, and when her boss was retiring she asked if she could be transferred to the White House for a temporary assignment; her wish was granted. She is currently on her way to fulfilling her lifelong dream. A dream she had at a very young age.

This is how to say YES, it is through your action; it isn't by screaming the words or chanting. You have to look for opportunities, say YES to change, and work towards it.

START WITH THE RIGHT ATTITUDE

The right attitude is the first step to a life of YES, once you have the right attitude about your circumstances; doors of favor begin to open. Your choices begin to align with your perception.

Your perceptions may begin to sprout to a better life and opportunities. Like the lady with one strand of hair that found a way to pack it up; your attitude is fundamental to the results you would attain.

Whatever you say YES to, you must start with the right attitude. "Be thankful that you don't already have everything you desire ... if you did, what would there be to look forward to?

Be thankful when you don't know something ... for it gives you the opportunity to learn. Be thankful for the difficult times ... during those times you grow. Be thankful for your limitations ... they give you opportunities for improvement. Be thankful for each new challenge... which will build your strength and character. Be thankful for your mistakes ... they will teach you valuable lessons. Be thankful when you're tired and weary ... because it means you've given your all. It's easy to be thankful for the 'good' things ... yet; a life of rich fulfillment comes to those who are thankful for the setbacks. Gratitude can turn a negative into a positive ... find a way to be thankful for your troubles and they can become your blessings." It is your attitude that matters. Always check your responses to the various happenings in your life and be determined to have a positive attitude about everything.

BE POSITIVE

"Words are singularly the most powerful force available to humanity. We can choose to use this force constructively with words of encouragement, or destructively using words of despair. Words have energy and power with the ability to help, to heal, to hinder, to hurt, to harm, to humiliate and to humble." Yehuda Berg

Be positive when difficulty comes. I had to make that choice last year. I could have picked despair, but I picked beauty; I chose gladness. I chose to look for my flicker of light. I began to speak life to my deadness. I chose to have a new perspective about my situation. Being positive is one way to say YES to living.

In my conversation with a Life Coach yesterday, I was inspired to share why I started Designed Life, and it got me thinking about a lot of things. Sometimes in life when you hit rock bottom, there is nowhere else to go but UP. You can at that moment re-create your life, and re-design your future.

It is believing. Transformations can only happen when we say yes to opportunities life offers.

Designing a new life is easy! You have to let go of the past, delete those things, processes, and relationships that don't fit into your new journey. This applies to every area of life. You can begin to command newness into your life. You can start PRAYING in the right people, the right opportunities! At that moment you stop faking PURPOSE, you BECOME A PURPOSE DRIVEN MAN OR WOMAN, a FORCE to be reckoned with, you simply BECOME! Your calling isn't what you do anymore; it BECOMES WHO YOU ARE.

LOOK FOR *YESortunities!*

Looking for YESortunities is looking for opportunities to say YES to. It means taking any YESortunities that comes your way that is aligned to your purpose. Giving yourself the freedom to accept change, and embrace the new things that come your way. It's not being afraid of failure because it does not exist. You must demand from life what you want from it; not timidly but with authority.

Knowing you have an inheritance in the vastness of this life that your foot has been planted in it for a reason. You have no reason not to have all that your heart desires. You have no reason to manage life, love, or circumstances. There is no better time to be alive than right now, this moment. You have been created for such a time as this, for this very moment. Don't settle for the mundane, fight for the extraordinary and BECOME!

Saying YES CAN Change your life

7

SAYING YES CAN CHANGE YOUR LIFE

Lend your ears to music, open your eyes to painting, and... stop thinking! Just ask yourself whether the work has enabled you to 'walk about' into a hitherto unknown world. If the answer is yes, what more do you want?

-Wassily Kandinsky

BY NOW YOU SHOULD BE SPEAKING THE UNIVERSAL LANGUAGE OF YES. By now I hope you are looking for YESortunities and are living life. I am certain that within this short time I have been able to teach you ways to say YES to life. I have taught you that accepting change enables you to say YES. I remembered a movie I watched years ago "Finding Nemo" about a fish who said YES to finding a world beyond his home, Nemo ended up lost but he learned so much along the way and finally made it back home. Saying YES is not staying in hurtful situations, or doing something that would hurt others. Even in that instance, however, we can still say Yes to the process of pain, hurt, and fear. YES is willing and accepting that we don't have the power over some experiences and we should just let it pass.

We are all addicted to being in control but saying YES lets us lose our guard and live life fully and unrestricted.

I remember when I was induced during childbirth because my body had re-fused to go into labor naturally. It was a very painful experience. I wanted to run away and leave the hospital bed, believing that would reduce the pain. I thought I was dying.

It was painful. After 16 hours of agonizing pain, I went through the pain of epidural, then a C-section surgery. And my beautiful baby was born, healthy, beautiful, and I forgot all about the pain. My son is now 5 1/2 years old, and I don't remember the pain I endured in order to bring him forth, only the scars remain. The second time around I was already a pro.

We all go through periods of loss, pain, hurt, etc. But it will end, you would smile again, you would grow. Your falling isn't your defeat but a stepping stone for your next level.

We are all addicted to being in control but saying YES lets us lose our guard and live life fully and unrestricted. In order to lead a full life, we need to open our hearts, so we can be completed by everything that is meant for us. We can birth new ideas, create new opportunities, love fully, learn new things by saying YES.

In an old episode of Whose Line is It Anyway, Johnstone writes: "Once you learn to accept offers, and then accidents can no longer interrupt the action. [...] This attitude makes for something really amazing in the theater. The actor who will accept anything that happens seems supernatural; it's the most marvelous thing about improvisation: you are suddenly in contact with people who are unbounded, whose imagination seems to function without limit."

[...]

These 'offer-block-accept' games have a use quite apart from actor training. People with dull lives often think that their lives are dull by chance. In reality, everyone chooses more or less what kind of events will happen to them by their conscious patterns of blocking and yielding.

When you begin to say YES, the world responds, events seem almost supernatural, and extraordinary. I have always told people that I am unbounded. I am limitless. I live my life that way. I am not afraid of opportunities. I started my business saying YES. In 2010, a lady walked up to me in church and asked if I could build a website. Of course, I said YES... The truth was that, I didn't know how to. I got paid for the job and started learning Adobe Dreamweaver as I go. I would call a dear friend, to help me out. It was crazy. In the end, I had to return her money. But guess what? I never backed down from the challenge. I went on to learn as much as could about building websites, a great tool that has helped my business till date.

In 2012, I kept paying someone else to design flyers, book covers, etc. for my clients. Sometimes I would use MS Word.... my printer hated it, but I made some money from it. So I taught myself how to use Photoshop, InDesign, etc.

I could go on and on about how I have said YES to clients or friends and in turn added value to my life. Hopefully as you begin to say YES to learning, new doors would open for you.

KEEP THIS IN MIND, IT HAS HELPED ME TREMENDOUSLY:

1. Be open to learning daily
2. Always say YES to new opportunities to expand your level of thinking.
3. Be creative
4. Build your skill set
5. Learn simple techniques that would enhance your business and life.
6. Research, research, research don't ever be clueless about a topic.

I said YES to book publishing when I didn't know too much about it, and that helped birth Eleviv Publishing Group. I said YES to inventing, as an African Women, and it has opened amazing doors that's on its way to make millions. I said Yes to textile design, and it helped birth Eleviv Textile, I said Yes to inventing new things, and much more, and it has transformed my life. Everything I have done with my life has

"Once you learn to accept offers, and then accidents can no longer interrupt the action.

been calculated choices fueled by YES. Creative people say YES, to newness and innovation. You have to walk in that same spirit. Don't be defined by fears and limitations. You are amazing, you are limitless, you are transcendent, you are God's most treasured creation, there's no one like you, none will ever be you, you have the ability to create and most importantly you have the right to say YES to amazing and new experiences.

I would end this book with a powerful quote by my favorite motivational speaker of all time, a quote that has changed my life, and it reads:

> *"If you want a thing bad enough to go out and fight for it, to work day and night for it, to give up your time, your peace and sleep for it… if all that you dream and scheme is about it, and life seems useless and worthless without it… if you gladly sweat for it and fret for it and plan for it and lose all your terror of the opposition for it…if you simply go after that thing that you want with all your capacity, strength and sagacity, faith hope and confidence and stern pertinacity…if neither cold, poverty, famine nor gout, sickness nor pain, of body and brain, can keep you away from the thing that you want…if dogged and grim you beseech and beset it, with the help of God, YOU WILL GET IT! – Les Brown*

START SAYING YES TO LIFE, TO LOVE, TO GOD…

XOXO

Vivian E.O

FIND OTHER BOOKS BY THE AUTHOR ON HER SITE

WWW.VIVIANOKOJIE.COM

UPCOMING BOOKS

- I CAN INVENT THINGS
- I AM BEAUTIFUL
- FINDING BEAUTY
- JIDEL'S JOURNEY
- 60 DAYS REFLECTION BOOKLET
- SONG OF SOLOMON (AN EPIC LOVE STORY)
- LIFE LESSONS COFFEE TABLE BOOK
- 10 WAYS TO UNLEASH YOUR CREATIVITY
- I MAKE SHIFT HAPPEN

My CONTACT Information

To Contact the Author visit her online
www.vivianokojie.com and email info@vivianokojie.com
You can also visit www.elevivllc.com or/and www.eleviv.co

To invite her to speak at your next conference or workshop call 713-730-5071 or email her.

Connect with her on:

Twitter @vivianelebiyo
Facebook @vivianelebiyo
LinkedIn @vivianelebiyo
Instagram @vivianelebiyo
Pinterest @vivianelebiyo

About VIVIAN ELEBIYO Okojie

Author, Motivational Speaker, Relationship Expert, Serial Entrepreneur, Movie Producer, Inventor, Talkshow host, and a Woman of Faith.

Vivian is the Executive Innovator and Co-owner of Eleviv Strategy Group a holding company for three other companies, Eleviv Publishing Group, Eleviv Textile, and Eleviv & Elessy.

Degrees in Business Administration: Florida A & M University, (2002) Business Information Technology, University of Phoenix (2012), Masters in Christian Counseling from the Center for Biblical Studies, A.S Public Relations (2000).

She is the writer/producer of a new movie "The Ultimate Commitment", a movie based on her book "Ready? Sex? Wait! The movie shows how one decision in our lives affects our seed which leads us on the quest of untraceable mines.

Vivian is a powerful and engaging speaker on the topic of goal setting, goal accomplishment, positive self-esteem, and abstinence which is the focus of her book, Ready? Sex? Wait!

Vivian Elebiyo has spoken at numerous venues including TBN, Department of Health Florida Abstinence Program, Churches, Schools, several radio stations, and events. Some of her written work has been featured in newspapers and several magazines. Vivian's goal is to empower others and motivate them to impact their world.

JOURNAL WORKBOOK

The big question is whether you are going to be able to say a hearty yes to your adventure.
-**Joseph Campbell**

SKILLS TO LEARN

(For Example: Sewing, Technical skills, Writing, etc.)

Type of Skills	TIMELINE TO LEARN		
	< 1 year	1-5 years	>5 years

FINANCIAL GOALS

(For Example: Get out of debt, investments, savings etc.)

Type of Financial Goals	TIMELINE		
	< 1 year	1-5years	>5 years

BUSINESS IDEAS

(Write down business ideas you can start, brainstorm solutions to problems, etc.)

Ideas	TIMELINE TO CREATE, PATENT, REGISTER, LAUNCH		
	< 1 year	1-6 years	>5 years

LIFE GOALS

Type of Goals	SPECIFIC GOALS		
FAMILY			
SPIRITUAL			
CAREER			
PHYSICAL			
SOCIAL			
MARRIAGE			
RELATIONSHIPS			

HUMANITARIAN			
EDUCATIONAL			
EMOTIONAL			

MY YES LIST

(WHAT I WOULD SAY YES TO)

NOTES